# Feminism
## FOR
## TEENAGERS

# DEDICATED TO
## Shree

Phototypeset from author's disk by Piccadilly Press.
Printed and bound by WBC, Bridgend
for the publishers Piccadilly Press Ltd.,
5 Castle Road, London NW1 8PR

A catalogue record for this book is available from the British Library

ISBNs: 1 85340 400 4 (hardback)
1 85340 405 5 (trade paperback)

*Cover illustration by Sophie Grillet*
*Cover design and typesetting by Paul Cooper Design*

*Sophie Grillet* was born, grew up, became a hippie and was thrown out of school in Cambridge. She went to art college in Brighton during the Punk era. She's been a freelance cartoonist ever since. She recently moved to Michigan, USA, where she lives with her husband and two very young sons.

# Feminism

## FOR
## TEENAGERS

# Sophie Grillet

Piccadilly Press • London

# CONTENTS

# CONTENTS

# WHAT IS FEMINISM?

For the purposes of this book, a feminist is a woman who has actively sought and fought for rights for women.

Lizzie Ahern

Inessa Armand

Hubertine Auclert

Dorothea Beale

Simone de Beauvoir

Vilma Espin

Lidia Falcon

Ichikawa Fusae

Artemesia Gentilleschi

Olympe de Gouges

Germaine Greer

Sylvia Pankhurst

Pandita Ramabai

Nawal El Saadawi

Sappho

Lucy Stone

Flora Tristan

Sojourner Truth

Wu Tsao

Virginia Woolf

Clara Zetkin

Thousands of women have contributed to the struggle for equality in many different ways, including women from the past, often rediscovered only recently by feminist historians, and women from other countries, often unheard of outside their own national borders.

# Why feminism's necessary

There are several theories...

## Theory 2 Men can fight

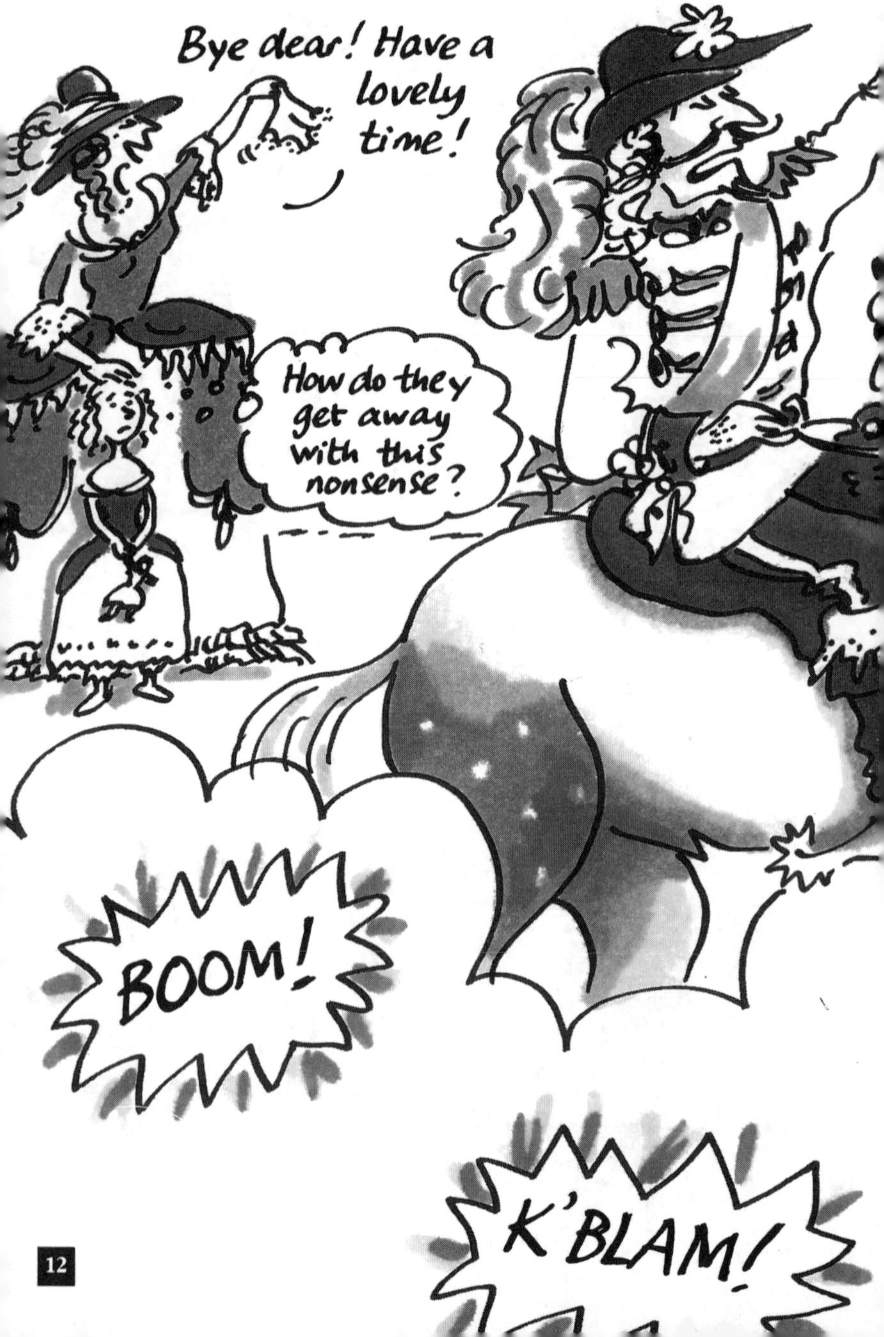

13

Women are not complete strangers to warfare, especially when defending their people from invading foreign armies.

A story from Apocrypha in the Bible tells of a widow called Judith who goes at night into the tent of Holofernes, the general of the Babylonian army which is besieging her people. She pretends to betray them but instead, she gets him drunk and cuts his throat.

Some military leaders who fought foreign invaders include:

**Boadicea**
This was the Roman name for Boudicca, Queen of the Iceni people in Britain. In AD60 she raised a revolt against the Romans throughout SE England after they forcibly annexed her land and raped her daughters. London and Colchester were burned down, but she failed to expel the invaders, and committed suicide.

**Joan of Arc** (1412-1431)
This is the English name for Jeanne d'Arc. In 1429, she persuaded Charles VII of France that she had a divine mission to drive the English out of France. She led a defeat of the English at Patay, but

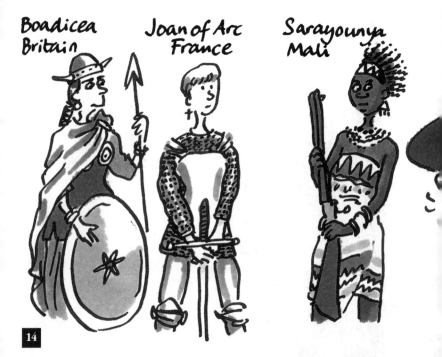

Boadicea
Britain

Joan of Arc
France

Sarayounya
Mali

was later captured and sold to them. An English-supporting tribunal of French churchmen found her guilty of witchcraft and she was burned to death in Rouen.

### Sarayounya of Mali

She was a tribal leader who was raised to know the skills of warfare. She led a revolt against the French colonial invaders in the 19th century, with some success in battle.

Women battalions fought in the Paris commune in 1871 and against General Franco's fascist army in the Spanish Civil War in 1936. Most infamously, women have been involved in bombing campaigns, as in the Algerian War of Independence (1954-63) and for the Irish Republican Army.

Armies prefer to recruit men for social, rather than biological reasons

Never forgetting...

Margaret Thatcher

Bomb the Argentine Ship, Belgrano!

We run the communal household, the children are ours, we make the food and we decide what God thinks. Today, she thinks it's time you caught more rabbits

OK. Right away

women of wife-group

Man of husband-group

As people learned to make things like bows and arrows, pottery and metalwork, they could produce more food and goods than were needed from day to day - enough for some of them not to work. This enabled them be priests or rulers, for example.

And also there's another theory that because women bear children they belong at home...

# CHAPTER ONE

# Domestic women

"A woman's place is in the home."

It starts when you sink in his arms...

...And ends with your arms in his sink.

What is it about me that says I should do all the housework I don't remember signing an agreement

## Some popular **MALE** excuses

"I've been working hard all day."

"I don't know how to clean the toilet, because I never have."

"Dirt doesn't bother me like it does you."

"I can't – I promised to meet my mates at the pub."

There was an old woman who lived in a shoe

Had so many children, she didn't know what to do

So she joined a campaign for free nursery ed.

And got a good job to help pay for their bread

Almost all the caring for young children is done by women.

Many women are caught in "the poverty trap" because of the lack of free or low-cost childcare.

## A change of mind

With a rapid expansion in education and contraception in the 1960s and 70s, many women started to question the idea that they should think of nothing more than getting married as young as possible, having children and staying at home to be a housewife and mother.

The introduction of Women's Studies in the 1970s really helped spread the knowledge of women's contributions through history.

**Mary Wollstonecraft** (1759-1797) wrote this book in 1792, inspired by Thomas Paine's *Rights of Man*. Her main concern was that girls should be educated. Her personal life was a mess, and she was constantly struggling to support herself by writing or teaching. She died following the birth of her second daughter.

"How many women thus waste life away the prey of discontent, who might have practised as physicians, regulated a farm, managed a shop, and stood erect, supported by their own industry..."

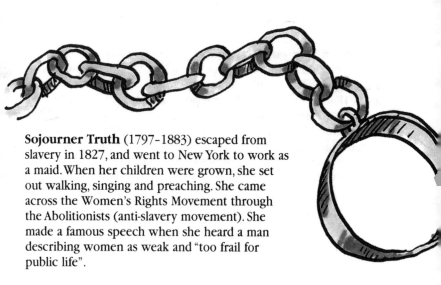

**Sojourner Truth** (1797-1883) escaped from slavery in 1827, and went to New York to work as a maid. When her children were grown, she set out walking, singing and preaching. She came across the Women's Rights Movement through the Abolitionists (anti-slavery movement). She made a famous speech when she heard a man describing women as weak and "too frail for public life".

I could work as much as a man, and bear the lash as well — and ain't I a woman?

**Sarah Mapp Douglass** (1806-1882) and **Lucretia Mott** (1793-1850) were schoolteachers, one black and one white, who with others, set up the Female Anti-Slavery Society in 1833. They were determined to stand up and speak, in spite of their meetings being attacked by racist mobs. Slavery was finally abolished in America in 1865.

**Susan B Anthony** (1820–1906) and **Elizabeth Cady Stanton** (1815–1902) Elizabeth was a judge's daughter who helped to organise the first Women's Rights convention in Seneca Falls, New York in 1848. It was a year of much political upheaval, and new ideas were gaining ground. She met up with Susan B Anthony, who travelled around organising and making speeches, while Elizabeth, who had eight children, mostly stayed home and wrote. They campaigned on violence as grounds for divorce, the vote, and women's working conditions.

All these women have fought for more equality — but some of them had five or more children to bring up, little or no education, and, unless they could afford servants, a prodigious amount of housework to do.

The black American writer, Alice Walker, remembers of her mother:

*"By the time she was 20, she had two children and was pregnant with a third. Five children later, I was born... Her quick, violent temper was on view only a few times a year, when she battled with the white landlord who had the misfortune to suggest that her children did not need to go to school.*

*"She made all the clothes we wore...all the towels and sheets we used. She spent the summers canning vegetables and fruits. She spent the winter evenings making quilts enough for our beds.*

*"During the 'working' day, she laboured beside - not behind - my father in the fields before sun up, and did not end until late at night. There was never a moment for her to sit down, undisturbed, to unravel her own private thoughts, never a time free from interruption by work or the noisy inquiries of her many children..."*

We may not be loveable, but we have allowed a transformation of women's lives

The Pill

But it obviously takes more than labour-saving devices to give women full social and psychological freedom and equality.

The family home is both a haven and a prison. People often feel trapped in roles they never chose. Sometimes it is even a place of violence or sexual abuse. But the current alternatives are such that most people choose to live in a family if they can.

Each battle won over ownership, the vote, contraception or other rights, helps to break down these barriers, but in the end some people benefit, and others think that things should be kept as they are. Imagine if women suddenly stopped caring for families in the home...

Hey! You're supposed to be on my side! Wouldn't we both benefit from free restaurants and launderettes – like we have free healthcare? And wouldn't we all be happier working only five hours a day?
SUN
Of course, but income tax would never cover it, and it wouldn't be right for us to decide what happens to the money companies make when we work for them, would it? Would it?
Dream
Dream
Free Door-to-door Nappy Service
FREE NURSERY
FREE
TIME!
FREE TAXI
FREE HOUSE CLEANIN SERV
FREE FURNITURE DEPOT

# Working women

Do our extreme differences in silhouette tell us something about the inequality of the Victorian age?
Yes.
I'm sorry - secretarial work is strictly for men. You'll have to wait until after the First World War
VACANCY
SECRETARY
What I need is a wife at home to look after the house and kids

# Why women work

Why do women feel they need to justify going to work? Because women have been made to feel that they're not a legitimate part of the workforce — that they should really be at home cooking elaborate dinners and letting repairmen in. Employers can exploit women's guilty feelings to treat us unequally.

# A history of women's work

*Just think - if there were machines to harvest the fields, preserve the fruit, and to spin, wash and sew, we women could put our feet up and relax!*

The Levellers, a radical political group in the English Revolution of the 17th century, used to say,

"When Adam delved, and Eve span,
Who was the gentleman?"

and they meant that everyone worked with no distinction between common and posh - but it also suggests a division of labour without men's labour being given greater value than women's.

I **like** being a spinster – a woman who earns her own keep by spinning – and doesn't rely on any man!

Wealthier women were administrators running large households. Like many women's jobs within the farm or household, it was unpaid, but nonetheless gave a sense of worth in the community.

I have to pay the butler, the cook, the ostler, the housekeeper, the maid, the skivvy, the butcher, the baker, the candlestickmaker, and we have 25 guests coming...

Not another blooming pearl to sew on

A very few women worked in skilled trades in the towns and cities, and many worked as low-paid seamstresses or lacemakers.

43

45

Did you find work?

No. Where are the children?

Jane's gone off with some young man. Henry and the baby are dead

Conditions were so appalling at the turn of the 18th century that Lord Shaftesbury believed, "Domestic life and discipline must soon be at an end; society will consist of individuals no longer grouped in families."

The "Luddites" broke up the machines which took their livelihoods, but they couldn't stop the pace of industrialisation when there were such vast profits to be made in the early years of the 19th century.

The worries of the more long-sighted parts of the ruling class about social instability, and workers' own worries about their families, coincided with demands for shorter working hours and other protective legislation. From the 1830s, these laws began to come in.

Faced with sex discrimination and laws meant to protect women from the toughest jobs, some women resorted to "personating" – dressing up as a man to get a job, for which they could be arrested.

## Trade Unions

As individuals we can do very little. Why don't we join one of these new Combinations of workers?

Shush! Aren't they against the law?

CACKA-CLACKA-CLACKA

Combinations or Trade Unions were made legal in 1824 (hedged about with restrictions) and many women joined, often in separate "lodges".

I don't want women in the Union! They only undercut our rates!

If we were paid the same as you to operate the new machines, it wouldn't happen! For that, we need to be in the Union.

Trying vainly to protect their dying crafts, the men were prone to sexist and racist ideas against the women and immigrants who were brought in to do their jobs. Weavers, whose craft had long been destroyed, were open to mixed Unions, and by 1876 nearly half their membership was female.

Mrs Emma Paterson thought women shouldn't be in men's unions anyway. She set up the Women's Protective and Provident League, which later became the Women's Trade Union League (WTUL) in 1874.

At the Trade Union Congress in 1876...

> I am opposed to cutting women's hours. Their wages will go down.

> What does she know? She's never worked long hours in industry. The Ten Hour Day Act of 1847 led to a cut in men's hours too

TUC 1876

> Wives should be in their proper place at home. It's working women's fault that in Manchester a quarter of all babies don't live to see their first birthday

As long ago as 1888 the TUC voted for a proposal for equal pay for women (put forward by the WTUL) but put no vigour into pursuing it.

Towards the end of the century, new general and unskilled unions began to appear, with slightly more egalitarian attitudes.

**Flora Tristan** (1803-1844) was the first person to think globally about Trade Unions and workers. She worked as a poorly-paid engraver's colourist in Paris and came up with the idea, "Workers of all countries unite!" inspiring Karl Marx.

Flora's Program included the recognition of every man and woman's right to work; moral, intellectual and vocational training for working class women, so they could improve the morals of men; and equality in law of men and women, as the only means of achieving the unity of humanity. She wanted to set up "Workers' Palaces", which would provide things like health care, schools and care for the elderly. She saw welfare provision as essential for women's freedom.

**Annie Besant** (1847-1933) was a socialist who is most famous for helping the "match girls" who made matches in Bow, East London. In 1888 she leafletted the factory and encouraged the women to walk out on strike. (Another famous feminist, Millicent Fawcett, was a shareholder, and so opposed the restriction in the use of yellow phosphorus, which was damaging the match girls' health.)

The publicity Annie Besant gave the strike, which quickly resulted in a pay rise and an end to fines and deductions, may have encouraged some others: women in a tin-box factory threw flour and red dye over men who wouldn't come out on strike with them; mill girls in Scotland came out over the poor quality of the yarn they were expected to work with, and wool weavers in the North of England rejected a pay cut, and marched in a procession headed by girls playing concertinas. The concertina players were arrested and fined for "obstruction". Women cigar makers, onion-skinners and tailors also went on strike with varying degrees of success. The tailors' strike, in Leeds, led to the formation of a new Union, the Society of Working Women, which grew to over two thousand members in a few weeks.

**Eleanor Marx** (1855-1898), Karl Marx's daughter, organised the first women's branch of the Gasworkers' Union in 1889.

Soon women's branches were increasingly amalgamated into the main unions. By 1896, there were almost 118,000 women in unions in Britain. One hundred years later, there are almost three and a half million.

51

# Women's work in wartime

With the First World War (1914-1918), women were suddenly welcome in jobs and professions that had previously excluded them, as the men went off to fight.

Because so many thousands of young men were killed in the war, and because prejudice had begun to break down a little as women proved that they could do the jobs, many carried on with them after the war. The middle classes were horrified at the sudden lack of domestic servants as women flocked to better work in factories, shops and offices.

I can only do this job because there's a nursery at work for my baby. D'you think they'll keep it going after the war?

**Equal Pay**

'Course they will. It's progress. Have you noticed all the women's magazines are suddenly full of ways to make cooking and housework quicker and easier?

Between the wars, in the 1930s, the terrible economic slump and high unemployment made improvements in the conditions of workers, male or female, hard to achieve. Equal pay was a long way off, in spite of an "Equal pay for equal work" meeting held in London in 1934 soon after unemployment had reached its peak.

But the ideal of "the rate for the job" - disregarding the gender of the person doing the job - was catching on. The engineering union voted in favour of it in 1935 - eight years before they agreed to admit women members.

Could it be true that women's work is to blame for unemployment? Is the international crisis of capitalism my fault?

Why be equal with me? I've got nowt

Here we are at war again, filling in for the men, doing their work, and we're still only getting half the pay!

I'll be calling for equal pay – to stop you undercutting us when we come home!

Unions began to demand equal pay and the government set up a Royal Commission on equal pay in 1944.

But by the 1950s, teachers and civil servants won equal pay. The European Economic Community, which did not yet include Britain, adopted equal pay as part of the Treaty of Rome in 1956.

~ A Royal Commission is something the Government sets up when they know everyone wants something, but they'd like to buy some time, and hope it gets quietly forgotten about

The Equal Pay Act was passed in 1970, but did not take effect until 1975.

The timescale gave employers years to dream up ways to evade the Act

There were several equal pay strikes in the early 1970s, many in protest at the men being given an extra £1 on the grounds that they might have to drive a forklift truck – something they never did.

Trade Union officials preferred women to go through equal pay tribunals. But the number of claims dropped off sharply after the first couple of years as women realised the Act was so riddled with loopholes that they rarely won.

Barbara Castle, whose act it was, and the British Institute of Management succeeded in unenthusing men in general and Trade Union officials in particular, by stating that any pay awards won by women would have to come, not out of profits, but out of the pockets of their male colleagues.

In 1996, women's pay was four-fifths of men's hourly rate. Part-timers (almost half of women employees) get less than two thirds of men's full-time hourly rate.

It's simple- you get equality with men if they let you do the same job men do. But, not being equal, they keep you in 'women's work'. So because you're not equal, you can't be equal, if you follow me

55

# Working women's problems

## Childcare

I'm a single parent, and virtually nothing is provided to help us out of poverty and into work

Many more women would go out to work, and for longer hours, if there was good childcare provision. In 1995, almost half of women with children under five worked, either full or part-time. But, without free nursery provision it often barely pays.

Children are treated as solely the responsibility of the parents, and in particular, the mother, although society would grind to a halt without a new generation.

I have three brothers, but if our aged mother needs care, it's me who's expected to take time off work. They earn more than me, but maybe that's because I'm seen as unreliable!

## Sexual harassement

Sexual harassment at work, whilst it can happen to both sexes, is primarily aimed at women, partly because it's really only a person in a position of power who can abuse it.

He threatened I'd lose my job, if I complained about his constant sexual comments and touching

At work, the way women dress is used against them.

Tribunals have found that women who complain of being forbidden to wear trousers to serve in a bookshop, or of being compelled to wear very tight, revealing clothes to do waitressing, are raising a trivial matter not worthy of judgement.

If I dress 'too femininely' I'm supposed to be inviting harassment, and not worthy of promotion. If I'm 'too businesslike', the boss thinks I'm not sufficiently decorative for promotion

## Recognition

Do women receive recognition at work? Usually they encounter a "glass ceiling" which prevents them from reaching the top positions. Only about 5% of women in Britain have broken through. In legal and medical practices, women often find less experienced men promoted to partner or senior partner.

Some women scientists have been recognised:
**Marie Curie** (1867-1934) jointly won the Nobel Prize for discovering Radium in 1911.

**Dorothy Hodgkin** (1910-1994) was a biochemist who won the Nobel Prize for the structure of penicillin in 1964.

Others have not:
**Lise Meitner** (1878-1968) discovered nuclear fission, for which Hahn received the Nobel Prize in 1944.

**Rosalind Franklin** (1920-1958) was a biophysicist who played a central role in discovering the structure of DNA, for which Crick, Watson and Wilson received the Nobel Prize in 1962.

**Jocelyn Bell Burnell** (1943-) is an astronomer who discovered pulsars, for which Hewish received the Nobel Prize in 1974.

# CHAPTER THREE

# Political women
## Queens

The most foolproof way to gain political influence is to be born with it. Although many royal families such as the British Royal Family discriminate against female succession, queens, whether ruthless or benevolent, at least are not ignored by history.

*Of course I'm a megalomaniac! As a god-queen, my people expect no less of me! My temple needs to be a bit enormouser. See to it.*

*Typical of your male-dominated age that I'm most famous for being in love with Anthony and looking like Elizabeth Taylor, rather than for ruling Egypt*

Queen Hatshepsut

Queen Cleopatra

With my husband, Ferdinand, I knocked Spain into shape — persecuted Jews, withdrew rights from Muslims, had troublemakers tortured by the Inquisition, and sent Christopher Columbus off to look for land and gold to grab.

Queen Isabella of Spain (1451-1504)

I decided not to risk getting married and sharing my power with a man. England flourished under me, by the slave trade, piracy, the secret police and wiping out the opposition (including my sister).

Queen Elizabeth I (1533-1603)

I became Queen after having my husband Peter III imprisoned (and murdered). Russia had huge numbers of serfs whose conditions I generally worsened. I spent the whole of my reign engaged in expansionist wars.

Catherine the Great of Russia 1762-96 reigned

That's queens for you. But one of the few other ways to gain power and independence was to be a nun — or a King's mistress!

# Campaigns

All campaigns for social advance and justice have involved the active participation of women.

But some campaigns were for the particular rights of women. Before the 19th century, these would necessarily be by women of some social standing to gain rights in relation to men of a similar social position.

## Property, education and marriage

At the beginning of Queen Victoria's reign, the case of Caroline Norton began the reform of laws on child custody and married women's property.

Caroline and her supporters campaigned until a law was passed in 1839 which gave some rights of custody to the mother of children under seven, and access to older children.

When my marriage to the Right Richard Norton split up, he took our three young children away. I found I had no right in law even to see them, nor did I have any rights in the family home, not even to furniture I had brought to the marriage.

I tried to earn some money by writing books, but found that anything I earned was his! When he started writing libellous things about me, the law didn't allow me to sue my husband.

JUSTICE FOR CAROLINE!

The property and custody laws kept many women trapped in miserable marriages, but it was not until 1857 that women could seek a divorce, and in the same year they gained at least the same limited property rights as single women.

**Barbara Bodichon** (1827-1891) and **Bessie Parkes** (1829-1925) were known as the "Ladies of Langham Place". They both came from radical, unconventional families. In 1856...

Married women gained the same property rights as single women the following year, and in 1870 an Act of Parliament allowed married women to keep their own earnings, rather than handing them over to their husbands.

Barbara and Bessie set up a women's employment project and a Ladies' Institute, which invited speakers like Elizabeth Blackwell to talk on education and professions for women.

*I was inspired by Elizabeth Blackwell, the first woman doctor in America. She didn't even like medicine, but thought there ought to be women doctors!*

*I needed plenty of inspiration because they wouldn't allow me into medical school or the lectures on dissection, so I had to study privately and cut up bodies in my bedroom!*

Elizabeth Garrett

**Elizabeth Garrett Anderson** (1836-1917) went on to help found the London School of Medicine, and became the first woman mayor in Britain. With the help of her campaigning, women were allowed to be doctors from 1876.

Widespread secondary education for girls didn't start until 1871, but soon after, Girton College, Cambridge was founded by women, for women in 1873, and in 1878 London University began to offer degrees for women.

*It's funny- we just take school for granted now - but imagine what life would be like for girls if we weren't allowed to go to school?!*

## The French Revolution

The storming of the Bastille prison in July of 1789 marks the beginning of the French Revolution, but the abolition of feudal privileges, serfdom (although not slavery in the colonies), and tax exemptions was not enough for the working class women of Paris. By October, they felt the National Assembly was backsliding...

WE'RE HUNGRY!

WE DEMAND BREAD!

No bread? Let them eat cake! (I never said that!)

Women attacked and killed some of the King's Swiss guard, and forced him back to Paris with his wife, Marie Antoinette, and his son.

**Olympe de Gouges** (1748-1793) was associated with the less radical "Girondins".

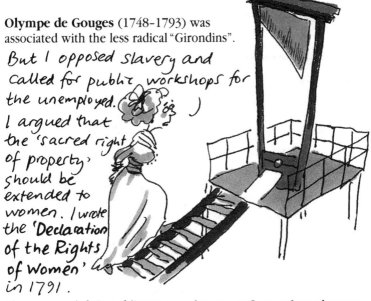

But I opposed slavery and called for public workshops for the unemployed. I argued that the 'sacred right of property' should be extended to women. I wrote the 'Declaration of the Rights of Women' in 1791.

The extreme left Republicans were known as *Sans-culottes* because the men wore trousers rather than the knee-breeches worn by the aristocracy. Some of the women, such as the club of Republican Revolutionary Women Citizens, also wore trousers and some even carried swords.

As the revolution degenerated they got into brawls with working class women in the marketplace, over whether they should wear the red Liberty bonnet.

We're not interested in the bourgeois 'sacred right of property'! We demand the vote! We demand equal job opportunities! Affordable food!

Legal and educational equality!

The revolution descended into Terror and Olympe de Gouges was guillotined, for declaring that she thought King Louis XVI shouldn't be.

By November 1793, the women's clubs were suppressed.

## The Paris Commune and Louise Michel

*Watch out!*
*The French Army is*
*trying to take our*
*cannon!*

With the fall of besieged Paris to the
Prussian Army in 1871, some of the
Parisian National Guard took all
their cannons to the workers'
district, out of the way of the
Prussians. But in the early hours of
18 March...

*Louise Michel*

**Louise Michel** (1830-1905) had
also led an armed attempt to
overthrow the useless Paris leaders
during the siege.

Milkmaids and other early risers surrounded the soldiers and
stopped them. Soon general rioting and insurrection broke out, and
in a few days the Government withdrew to Versailles, and the
Commune was declared. The Commune was the most democratic
system ever devised, with public officials paid the same as
ordinary workers, and elected representatives subject to
instant recall.

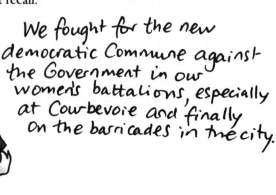

*We fought for the new*
*democratic Commune against*
*the Government in our*
*women's battalions, especially*
*at Courbevoie and finally*
*on the barricades in the city.*

Paris was bombarded by the French Army and the Commune ended, drowned in blood. Louise Michel was deported to Noumea and her comrade-in-arms, Elisabeth Dimitrieff, escaped, eventually to end her life with her exiled husband in Siberia. On her return, Louise Michel continued to be politically active and was frequently arrested. She died in London, overjoyed to hear about the first Russian Revolution of 1905.

## The Russian Revolution

Women textile workers who took to the streets in demonstrations in February 1917 were followed soon after by hungry women demanding bread and herrings. They smashed up a few buses and looted a few shops. From these humble beginnings, strikes and demonstrations soon led to the overthrow of the Czar and eventually the October revolution.

For the first time, many social provisions which could lift the extra burden from women were put into place. Free nurseries and laundries, free education and cheap cafeterias were set up. Abortion and homosexuality were legalised, and divorce was easy to obtain. Two months' paid maternity leave was given, and wife beating was outlawed.

Russia, a poor country even before fighting the First World War and the invasion of several foreign armies after the revolution, suffered a devastating famine. People were reduced to cannibalism in some parts of the countryside.

Lenin died in January 1924 and Joseph Stalin was in full control by the late 20s...

## Two activists

While Russia had a revolution, Germany also teetered on the brink of one. For several years, women in Germany were forbidden by law from taking part in politics.

**Clara Zetkin** abandoned her comfortable, middle class life to join the workers' movement, attending meetings that were often broken up by police. She worked endlessly to get women involved in campaigns to improve their lives, and ultimately in revolution, which she believed would bring liberation for women.

I came to Paris in 1881 when my boyfriend Ossip was exiled here. We had two sons, but we both fell ill from overwork, and Ossip died

Clara Zetkin 1857-1933

Her mother felt sorry for her and invited her home to Leipzig to recuperate, but couldn't persuade Clara to abandon her ideals. She attended secret meetings in Leipzig, and became more enthusiastic than ever about attracting women into political activity.

I've edited this paper for women for 25 years, since 1891. But much of my work is persuading **men** in Trade Unions and Socialist parties to listen to the needs of women. I've argued with Lenin about it. I'm a friend of his wife Nadezhda, you know.

*Gleichheit*

*Clara Zetkin*

In Japan it was also against the law for women to take part in politics. In 1918, **Ichikawa Fusae** (1893–1981) co-founded the New Women's Association to protest. She started out as a village teacher, but was soon leading campaigns for women workers for the International Labour Organisation.

Not all Japanese favoured our totalitarian government and its militarism. I was against it, and when the war was over, I started campaigning for women to have the vote.

Ichikawa was elected to the Upper House in the Japanese parliament in 1952 and continued to be re-elected with the support of women and radical groups, with hardly a break, until a very advanced age.

# Towards the vote

The Chartist movement in Britain in the 1830s demanded the vote for all adult men; that the ballot should be secret; that elections should take place every year; and that there should be no property qualification to becoming an MP. William Lovett had included women in the first draft of the Chartist petition and letters from women were sent to Chartist newspapers, saying women should be included in "universal suffrage", but the other male leaders decided this would make it harder to win.

The first Female Charter Association sprang up in Birmingham in 1838, its membership soon reaching 1,300.

Woman can no longer remain in her domestic sphere, for her home has been made cheerless her hearth comfortless and her position degrading... Woman's circle has been invaded by hired bands of police ruffians - her husband dragged from her side to the gloom of the dungeon - and her children trampled underfoot

It was not until 1865 that MP John Stuart Mill (1806-73) presented a Woman's Suffrage Bill, urged on by a petition organised by the "Ladies of Langham Place". His Bill was unsuccessful, but soon after he wrote *The Subjection of Women*.

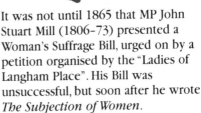

Women should have equality in all areas of life. I'm sure it will take a mass movement to achieve it

## The Suffragettes

**Emmeline Pankhurst** (1858-1928) came from Manchester, but went to school in Paris at the age of 13, in 1871 just after the Paris Commune ended.

Emmeline married a socialist campaigner who died when her daughters were still young. **Christabel** (1880-1958) and **Sylvia** (1882-1960) followed their parents into socialist feminist politics.

The Prime Minister himself says if we don't cause any trouble for the coronation, he'll most likely grant propertied women the vote in 1912

What a patronising con artist! Where's our VOTE?!

Dissatisfied with the Independent Labour Party's progress on Women's Rights, Emmeline set up the Women's Social and Political Union in Manchester in 1903.

Christabel and Sylvia set up branches of the WSPU in London. By 1907 there were 3000 branches nationally, and their paper, *Votes For Women*, sold 40,000 copies a week.

Arrested suffragettes went on hunger strike, and suffered the torture of force-feeding through a pipe pushed down their throats. The public outcry made the Liberal Government abandon force-feeding, and instead bring in the "Cat and Mouse Act" which allowed the hunger striking women to be released temporarily until they were well enough to be re-imprisoned. The campaigners used to keep their spirits up by leading all the prisoners in singing suffragette songs. Emmeline was sent to Holloway prison a dozen times, becoming extremely ill and exhausted.

This campaign is smashing!

(Overarm bowling in cricket was invented by Christina Willes)

Mama and I don't want your East London Federation in the WSPU
But working women have the strength and organisation to gain the vote and other social improvements
Christabel
Sylvia
Mama says working women are the **weakest** of our sex. We want only the very **best** pick for our window smashing and arson attacks

While Christabel and Emmeline became such strong patriots –
even the name of *Votes For Women* was changed to *The Britannia*
– Sylvia joined the anti-war Women's International League. About ten
million people from all countries died in the war, and maybe twice
that number were wounded.

It's easy to support Sylvia now, but which side do you take if your country goes to war?

HOORAH! WE WON.

Women over 30 can now vote. The others will soon follow!

At the end of the war in 1918, a time of huge social unrest, some women at last won the right to vote.

Emmeline joined the Conservative Party in 1926, the year of the General Strike, and stood as a parliamentary candidate.

VOTES FOR WOMEN

BALLOT BOX

New Zealand women had been first to win the vote in 1893, and many other countries soon followed. The last state in the USA finally agreed to female suffrage in 1920. In Switzerland, women couldn't take part in federal elections until 1971. In some countries, such as Kuwait and Saudi Arabia, women are still waiting.

The Nobel Peace Prize winner, **Rigoberta Menchu** (1959-) is a Quiche Indian from Guatemala who has fought for the rights of the indigenous people, including the right to vote, which was restricted to Guatemalans of Spanish descent. Both her parents and a brother were tortured and killed by the regime.

# Women in parliament

The first woman to be elected to the British parliament was **Countess Constance Markiewicz** (1868-1927). She was a leading member of Sinn Fein, seeking Home Rule for Ireland. She had been sentenced to death for her part in the Easter Rising of 1916, but it was commuted and she was released from prison in 1917.

She was elected in 1918, but did not take up her seat, to show that she thought the British parliament should not be passing laws for Ireland.

**Nancy, Lady Astor** (1879-1964) was the first woman MP to take up her seat in the British House of Commons. She took over as Conservative MP for Plymouth from her husband when he became a Viscount and went into the House of Lords in 1919.

Women still make up only a small minority of MPs. The hours and the "Gentleman's club" atmosphere discourage many from standing. Many countries have now had a woman Prime Minister or even President, not least Muslim countries like Turkey, Pakistan and Bangladesh. Israel and Sri Lanka led the way, with Golda Meir and Mrs Bandarinaika. Since then Iceland, India, the Philippines, Nicaragua and Ireland have been among those to join the club.

When Margaret Thatcher won the leadership of the Conservative Party, I cheered and voted for her in 1979, simply because she was a woman. I was very disappointed when she did nothing for us

Maybe you have to be pretty tough and heartless to claw your way up to a leadership position. And doubly so, if you're female!

# CHAPTER FOUR

# Physical Women
## Women and sexuality

Disgusting! How can you put those two words next to each other?

He only uses my services twice a week!

Phwoor! Women! Sex! It's what they're good for!

We're not going to be crudely defined by men as Madonnas or whores any more!

## Reproductive rights

Being able to decide when, whether, and with whom to have children is fundamental to the liberation of women. It means they have some control over their work, studies, sex life and bodies, without being told how to live by the government (invariably male dominated) or religious groups (invariably male led).

## Birth control

Methods of birth control have been practised for centuries, although none were as effective as modern methods.

The strengthening of The Church in the Middle Ages, and the witch hunts that accompanied it, meant a devastating loss of unwritten knowledge kept by women about contraception and abortion, besides techniques for easing childbirth.

*Thousands* of women across Europe were hanged or burnt at the stake as witches, often for practising herbal medicine.

Birth control was a taboo subject. When I wrote a guide to birth control, 'Married Love' in 1918, the book was considered scandalous.

Coming from Scotland, I also founded the first Birth Control clinic in London in 1921

**Marie Stopes** (1880–1958)

In 1927, a newlywed named Rose Kerrigan went to the birth control clinic in Glasgow to ask for contraception. She found they were horrified because they had never had a woman who did not yet have children come in and ask for contraception.

Many early birth control proponents were eager to prevent the lower classes from breeding too much. Some had links to the "Eugenics" movement, which wanted only the kind of white, middle class people they approved of to have lots of children.

Now they want to prevent people in poor countries from 'breeding' too much. But in spite of their offensive attitude, we want the chance to control our lives, like any other families.

Under Prime Minister Indira Gandhi, in the 1970s, there was a programme of sterilisation to try and curb the population which _____ practically forced men to have a vasectomy

The U.S. Agency for International Development was responsible in the 1970s for the sterilisation of over one third of Puerto Rican women of childbearing age

The modern equivalent is the population control argument, which is not applied to the rich, white countries. Starvation is not caused by population size, but the reasons why will have to be left to other books.

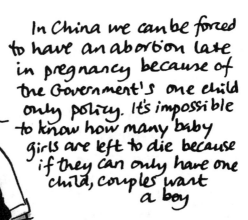

In China we can be forced to have an abortion late in pregnancy because of the Government's one child only policy. It's impossible to know how many baby girls are left to die because if they can only have one child, couples want a boy

89

*It seems every other government finds it necessary to tell women they either **must** or **must not** have as many or few children as they want*

## Abortion

In the mid-19th century, abortion was outlawed in Europe and the USA. Since the middle of the 20th century, it has been the subject of endless campaigns.

Abortion was legalised in Britain (though not Northern Ireland or Guernsey) in 1967, after a Bill was introduced by a Liberal MP. By 1988 there had been 15 unsuccessful attempts to limit the terms of the 1967 Abortion Act. Each time, big campaigns were able to protect the right of women to some choice.

In 1990, parliament agreed that the time limit on abortions should be reduced from 28 to 24 weeks.

*NOT THE CHURCH NOT THE STATE...*

*...WOMEN MUST DECIDE THEIR FATE!*

*Trade Unions joined in and demonstrated because we think the right to choose abortion is a class issue— wealthy women can always go to a discreet private clinic*

*They didn't seem to grasp that abortions are always carried out for extreme reasons, and late abortions particularly so. The Labour Party failed to defend working class women*

In the United States, abortion is a constant political battleground. Doctors who carry out abortions have been attacked and even murdered. Clinics have been bombed. The law varies widely between states: Pennsylvania requires parental consent to abortion for girls under 18, although the age of consent to sex is 14.

Abortion is illegal and punishable by imprisonment in 65 countries, some even in cases of rape or incest. It is impossible to know how many women have committed suicide because they could not have an abortion, or died from illegal, insanitary abortions. The World Health Organisation estimates that out of every half a million maternal deaths, 70,000 are caused by unsafe abortions.

Can you believe it would be the same if it were a problem faced by men—especially male legislators! The Government, the Church and various extremists fight for control over my internal organs. As long as women can be forced to bear an unwanted child – we can never be equal

We still have of our bodies, our own wombs.

don't control own

Many anti-abortionists oppose the use of contraception. Others pretend that contraception, besides being exclusively the woman's responsibility, is fail-safe. They generally oppose choices such as the drug RU486, or the "morning after pill" which make abortion possible at a much earlier stage of foetal development.

They tell us to lie on our backs, curl up in a ball, hold our breath and somehow squirt the baby upwards

Baby trajectory

Speaking from personal experience, the author finds this to be the exact opposite of what would make sense. In less medically dominated cultures, women normally squat or are supported by others in an upright position. But that would be inconvenient for a doctor wishing to have a look or prod around.

Technological advances, not least knowledge about hygiene, have transformed childbirth. They may often be inappropriately used, but at least the once common tragedy of death in childbirth is now rare.

# Rape and Other Violence against women

Sometimes the most oppressive aspect of being a woman is the threat of violence. It's hard to remember that more men than women are attacked on the streets, or that men can be victims of rape, especially in prison

Violence in the home or wife-battering is at last beginning to be taken seriously as a crime, though not in all countries. Being battered often creates low self-esteem in women which, along with financial dependence and the lack of anywhere to escape to, makes it hard to break the cycle of violence. Shelters for battered women, pioneered by Erin Pizzey in the 1970s, although too few, are a big help. They also compelled the public to see that the problem was widespread.

In India an even more frightening phenomenon is bride-burning. The husband's family murders the young bride if they are not happy with the value of her dowry

We are campaigning vigorously for prosecutions when it happens, and to make it socially unacceptable

In some East African countries, female circumcision is carried out. This is a form of genital mutilation on girls to cut off the clitoris, with the intention that, as women, they will get no pleasure from sex, and therefore be faithful to their husbands. Often the painful operation is done in very unsanitary conditions.

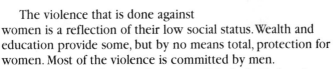

*Besides being barbaric, it's stupid — there's no understanding of human emotion or sexual response —*

In Britain it was finally accepted in 1991 that rape within marriage was unlawful. But of all rape accusations that came to trial in 1995, only a tenth led to a conviction. The law is necessary but not very helpful. Attitudes to women are far more critical in reducing rape.

The violence that is done against women is a reflection of their low social status. Wealth and education provide some, but by no means total, protection for women. Most of the violence is committed by men.

But mothers-in-law may be responsible for bride-burnings, and mothers may take their daughters to the medicine-woman for circumcision or to the Madam at the brothel to be sold into prostitution.

The problem is one of the whole of society's attitude to women, and of the violence within society as a whole.

# Body image

"You can never be too rich or too thin." - Duchess of Windsor

When a group of women who had married during the Second World War had a reunion, they put on their original wedding dresses, which fitted perfectly. Reporters asked, amazed, "Haven't you put on weight?" Their response was that in those days there was no pressure to be particularly thin. The same is certainly not true today.

Well you have to be thin, don't you- otherwise you're disgusting

what other outrageous prejudices do you have about people's physical appearance?

In spite of strong evidence that dieting damages the metabolism and makes it impossible for the body to regulate its weight naturally, millions of people spend much of their lives "on a diet". The compulsion to slim is starting among younger and younger children. The alarmingly constrictive corsets of a century ago, which were banished by an earlier generation of feminists, have been internalised. Is a mental corset better or worse?

One of the delightful aspects of the social upheavals of the late 1960s was the discovery that all kinds of shapes and colours of body could be considered beautiful. It happened again to a degree with the Punk movement in the late 1970s.

## Sex and Love

How do women see themselves depicted in films, on TV and in magazines? Mainly as very thin, passive "beauties", waiting to have sex done to them. In discussions of pornography, distinction is rarely made between supposedly consenting sex and rape.

When they say 'hard core', do they mean the male organ is on view, or do they mean grotesque violence? Is there no distinction?

Men think it's very rude when their sex organs are on display. It's all from a male perspective

It's true that the severest censorship is of sex from a woman's point of view

we no longer have a point of view. It's been stolen. All we are given is soppy romance

In the pre-industrial age, the complaint about women's sexuality was that they were far too "lustful", and were always too demanding for men. All recent studies show that to be far from the present truth. One survey asked women why they didn't make the first move in bed. The overwhelming response was that they "couldn't be bothered".

Although marriage is still popular, increasing numbers of couples are living together without marrying. A quarter of unmarried women under 50 are now co-habiting. The stigma against children born of such couples has melted away entirely in the cities, and barely remains elsewhere.

In Belgium, a country thought to be deeply conservative in its social views, couples started living together rather than marrying as soon as the tax laws altered to favour the arrangement financially over marriage.

Marriage, marriage... what about the ideal of FREE LOVE?!

Marriage, contrary to popular belief, must be more dear to men than women, as women are the more frequent instigators of divorce, and men are more likely to die soon after their spouse dies. Married women are more likely to suffer depression and low self-esteem than their single sisters.

In times of social change, the idea of love untied by permanent monogamous bonds always comes bubbling to the surface.

Yes, but men don't get pregnant. And in an unequal society, it often turns out to be just an excuse for men to get their leg over, then treat you like dirt. (Not that women invariably behave sweetly and lovingly to a one-night stand!)

But we have a society in which women are more emotionally vulnerable, having been taught to invest all in their emotions. Men are taught to ignore theirs as much as they can.

I have a dream that there'll come a day when it doesn't just lead to heartbreak and venereal disease

## Lesbians

Love and sex for women does not always involve men. The poet Sappho (612–580 BC) led a group of women writers on the island of Lesbos, from which the word "lesbian" comes.

Through most of history, women's love for one another has been a hidden experience because men didn't bother their heads about it. Passionate friendships between women such as the writer Charlotte Bronte and Ellen Nussey, involving kissing and going to bed together, were unremarked upon by men.

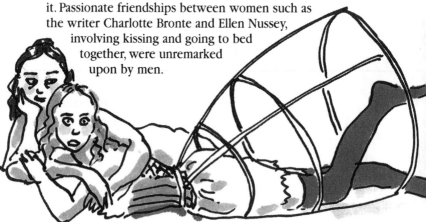

When women began to demand their rights in the 19th century, at a time when the new ideal of the middle class family was being rammed down our throats, a conflict arose. Only then was lesbianism defined, and of course plans were soon afoot to outlaw it. But Queen Victoria refused to agree to the Bill, saying such a thing couldn't possibly exist!

Another failed attempt was made to outlaw lesbianism in 1921, in spite of the misgivings of the Director of Public Prosecutions who thought it a big mistake to "let the whole world know that there *is* such an offence".

The women's movement in the 1960s was as hostile to us as everyone else, at first. But gradually, along with gay men, it's become a little easier to 'come out' and be accepted. Many people still view us with suspicion, for no particular reason.

Some people think there's no problem because you can hide your feelings...

... But apart from the stress of pretending not to be yourself, you can have your children taken from you, be refused a job, or be denied the benefits heterosexuals get from their partners' jobs.

A few feminists, mainly in the 1970s and 1980s, decided that sleeping with men was "sleeping with the enemy" and became "political lesbians". But most lesbians are simply women who fall in love with other women.

If it was easier to be gay, it is possible that many more people would open their minds to loving their own sex, whether always or occasionally.

## Romantic love

Romantic love was conceived in the 12th century and was strictly for the upper classes. It was not related to marriage but was about young knights swooning over married ladies and doing feats for (non-sexual) favours.

Marriage was a contract between families – the feelings of the individuals would be taken more or less into account according to the importance of the contract (eg cementing a peace treaty) and the soft-heartedness of the parents.

Let down your golden hair! And the key!

Expensive church weddings took a long time to catch on with the common people, who were more likely to go through a ceremony involving jumping over a broomstick. The broomstick, a phallic symbol, was also strongly associated with witches, who perhaps as priestesses of the Old Religion, were involved in the ceremony. The practice went on long enough to be recorded in the words of an American rock 'n' roll song, *"Come on baby, let's jump the broomstick, come on let's tie the knot."*

## Some writers

Soon after the Russian Revolution, **Alexandra Kollontai** (1872-1952) wrote that *"mankind today is living through an acute sexual crisis."* She asks, *"How can we explain...the way in which sexual problems are relegated to the realm of private matters that are not worth the effort and attention of the collective?"*

She tries to explain why people moan and pine for "great love": *"We live and think under the heavy hand of an unavoidable loneliness of spirit...Because of their loneliness people are apt to cling in a predatory and unhealthy way to illusions about finding a 'soul mate' from among the members of the opposite sex."* The problem with this, she says, is that *"the crude individualism that adorns our era is perhaps nowhere as blatant as in the organisation of sexual relationships. A person...naively imagines that being 'in love' gives them the right to the soul of the other person...To be rid of the ever-present threat of loneliness, we demand the right to know every secret of this person's being. The modern lover would forgive physical unfaithfulness sooner than 'spiritual' unfaithfulness, seeing any emotions experienced outside the 'free' relationships as the loss of their own personal treasure."*

**Simone de Beauvoir** (1908-1986) wrote *The Second Sex* in France in 1949. It was a detailed attempt to describe the emotional effect on women of their second-class status, and the way in which that oppression came about and operated. She challenged the universal notion that men are people and women are women. It was written at a time when nothing of the kind had been attempted, and had an enormous impact.

**Betty Friedan** (1921- ), an American, put her finger on the Problem Without A Name. She was writing in 1963 when life for middle class American women was at its most boring and constrictive. But her book, *The Feminine Mystique,* had resonances outside the American suburban housewife's circle, as the lost ideas of feminism began to resurface in the "second wave".

**Germaine Greer** (1939- ), an Australian writing in Britain, crashed onto the scene with her furious book, *The Female Eunuch* (1970). She was gloriously outraged by the degradation of women, and the way in which they had come to fear their own bodies.

A flood of publications followed, from Kate Millet's *Sexual Politics* (1970), which set out the theory of patriarchy as the root of women's oppression, and Michele Barrett's criticism of her, to Shere Hite's detailed surveys of women's sexual response.

# CHAPTER FIVE

# The battle goes on...

## "I'm not a feminist, but..."

I agree with most of this book – but I'm not a feminist!

Are you sure you haven't fallen for the 'feminist backlash'...

– those people who for more than a century have been portraying women who fight for their rights as ugly, 'man-hating' monsters?

Mind you – if you're ugly and you hate men –

I don't see why you can't fight for your rights! If you're pretty they ignore your views, and if not – that's a reason to ignore them too! I haven't noticed **men** having to pass a beauty test!

Fem for Teens

# Equality With Whom?

Feminists have had varying attitudes to men. I preferred it when we used the term 'women's liberation.' It seems most feminist writers today think inequality comes about because all men have 'power' over all women, and are horrible to women by choice or nature. This is the basis of 'patriarchy theory'.

UNEMPLOYMENT OFFICE

If we have so much power, how come we're even more likely to be laid off work than women?

I could do with being equal to some rich businesswoman! What they're really talking about is equality with men of their own class — and forget everyone else!

A survey in Japan showed that what Japanese working men most wanted to be (after a bird) was – a woman!

In many parts of the world, the improvements women need in their lives are not obviously in relation to men at all. A nearby source of clean water; a local school; a free clinic; cheap, readily available contraception; a bank that will lend small sums of money to women at very low interest; these are all more important to them.

Yes, but will the school take girls? If we have to pay, the boys' education will come first. And are they going to come up with some nonsense about contraception undermining manhood?

Yes, and will our husbands take the money we borrow away from us? Will they take our interest repayments so we go hungry if we pay the money back?

Sometimes the only way is to organise our own community schools or kitchens or loan schemes. But it's tiring having to do things which would be more efficient on a large scale, and it's tiring having to be constantly on our guard against men. They should be helping us.

## What feminism Means For Men

Women shouldn't try to be like men – not that they ever could. The liberated ones are OK for sex but I wouldn't want to marry one!

You've been reading too many tabloid newspapers! I suppose you thought it was great when men couldn't push a pram in public, or they'd be laughed at, or when little boys were expected not to cry if their mother died. I suppose you'd like to see sex roles so rigid that gay men and lesbians had to spend their whole lives in hiding, feeling guilty?

I don't want some homo touching me up!

Tell me you've never made any unwanted sexual advances, and I might sympathise

Men have a lot to gain from equality — things like paternity leave, and their womenfolk bringing in higher wages, but all they think about is having to share housework (why not?) and having women 'steal their jobs'.

Men have as much, or more to gain from peace and a clean environment, but they've often led to see these things as threats to 'their' jobs

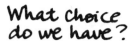

What choice do we have?

Who wants to choose between working in an armaments factory, and unemployment? Or to risk the sack by complaining of your employer's bad environmental practices?

113

I'll let him think it's 'his' job to steal, so he won't join forces with the women to get shorter hours or equal pay... then I'll give him the **sack!** Ha! Ha! Ha!

Although women are very gradually moving into some traditionally "male" jobs, men are not taking up traditionally "female" jobs. Unluckily for them, the number of "male" jobs has been declining (especially unskilled), while "female" ones increase.

Unemployed men have less chance of getting married, and a greater chance of falling into crime. Job discrimination is hurting men, too.

There's no advantage to women in having large groups of young, uneducated, unemployed young men, who will be attracted to drugs and gang life. It's not 'our loss is your gain'—forget the battle of the sexes!

Boys and girls are brought up differently from the day they are born.

Boys are excluded from certain pursuits as vigorously as girls are excluded from others...

While many mothers complain that fathers spend little time caring for young children, many fathers complain that with working overtime, they never see their children.

For men, building up relationships with their families has to be done in snatched moments on busy weekends.

Japanese senryu poem:
　　Long commute.
　　Morning stars, evening stars.
　　Child's sleeping face.

Discrimination hurts men too.

# Rights still to be won

- Women as property
- Women's property
- Education
- The vote
- Personal bank accounts
- Legal abortion
- Equal pay legislation
- Recognition of rape in marriage

But it's also true we've a long way to go. Sometimes it's impossible even to imagine real freedom, in the details or in general. Women's bodies are often seen purely in terms of men's sexual attitudes.

119

But I'm not sexist – I don't mind advertising a job at a lower rate of pay to attract more female applicants...

... and I don't mind a token woman on the board, so long as she agrees with me about divide and rule on the shop floor – no expensive perks or pay rises for women workers

I managed to get promoted to the board, but I still have to pretend I was stuck in traffic, rather than sorting out a child-care problem if I'm late.

They moan at working mothers, but where's the time off for parents to care for sick children?

They still think children should be seen but not heard of!

Equal pay legislation is riddled with loopholes, and has done little to end pay differences between men and women, especially as the kind of work done by each continues to be separate.

### Education

Girls do better than boys at school in Europe and America. At university, boys still have the edge, but probably not for long. In the USA, more girls than boys get a college education.

Once the barriers to female education are removed, girls do as well or, usually, better than boys. The 11+ exam used to mark girls down to make the exam "fairer" for "slower-maturing" boys. In Britain, girls score higher in tests at ages five, seven, nine and eleven. But the psychological barrier to maths and science still stands.

In the 18th century, ladies used to attend public science lectures out of interest.

123

# Who is the most oppressed?

A competition to be the most oppressed, or worse, a competition *between* the oppressed, achieves nothing. Naturally, some people respond to the injustice of prejudice by wishing to describe it in detail. This can be a lot more helpful, possibly convincing doubters but more usefully, spurring people into action. Any woman can describe oppression. The point, however, is to *end* it.

# Down with sexism!

Nothing changes unless people change it. There are no shortages of injustices - pick one from this book, or your own personal bugbear, and decide to try and do something about it. Find out if anyone else is already tackling the problem and join forces.

# Epilogue

The babe in the manger awoke
As the Magi made their entrance
Minding their silk shoes on the stable floor
Miraculously, the babe arose
Swaddled in pink terry towelling
She spake
'I am the Messiah,' she said
'Oh sorry, wrong stable,' muttered the Magi
Sheepishly making their way out
Through the press of kneeling animals
'Excuse me, beg pardon, Dobbin,'
'Oh myrrh,' said the babe in irritation
Hearing the farts of the departing camels
Until she remembered her elevated position.

# INDEX

# Bibliography

Asian Women Writers' Workshop: *Right of Way: Prose and Poetry*
(Women's Press, 1988)

de Beauvoir, Simone: *The Second Sex*
(David Campbell, 1993)

Charlesworth, Kate and Marsaili Cameron: *All That – the other half of history*
(Pandora Press, 1986)

Greer, Germaine: *The Female Eunuch*
(Paladin, 1971)

Orbach, Susie: *Fat is a Feminist Issue*
(Paddington Press, 1978)

Rowbotham, Sheila: *Hidden from History: 300 Years of Women's Oppression and the fight against it*
(Pluto Press, 1977)

Schneir, Miriam, ed: *The Vintage Book of Feminism*
(Vintage, 1994)
*The Vintage Book of Historical Feminism*
(Vintage, 1996)

Spender, Dale: *Man Made Language*
(Pandora Press, 1990)

Walker, Alice: *The Colour Purple*
(Women's Press, 1983)

Watkins, Susan, Marisa Rueda and Marta Rodriguez: *Feminism for Beginners*
(Icon Books, 1992)

Winterson, Jeanette: *Oranges are not the Only Fruit*
(Vintage, 1990)

Wolf, Naomi: *The Beauty Myth*
    (Vintage Books, 1991)

Woolf, Virginia: *A Room of One's Own*
    (Chatto & Windus, 1984)

Film:      *Rosie the Riveter*, 1944, Joseph Santley
          *The Life and Times of Rosie the Riveter*, 1988, Connie Field

Website: http://www.netsrq.com/~dbois/
          Distinguished women of past and present

# SPIN THE BOTTLE

## James Pope

Zoe is in trouble for skipping school, fighting, smoking, messing around in class . . .

Sally Ward, her form teacher, tries to deal with Zoe's outrageous sense of humour and help her through the year. Sally suggests using their computers as a two-way journal, a means of exchanging thoughts over the problems Zoe is facing.

However, Sally finds that Zoe's problems go far, far deeper than she could ever imagine. For Zoe is hiding a tragic secret . . .

*" a thought-provoking story . . ."* – Books Magazine

*"A little gem to while away those cold winter nights!"* – Mizz

## SEX: HOW? WHY? WHAT?
### The Teenager's Guide

## Jane Goldman

**How** . . . do you French kiss?
do you put on a condom?
do you make love?

**Why** . . . is it important to care about your sexual partner?
is masturbation a great idea?
do you have crushes on unavailable people?

**What** . . . the heck is going on with your body during puberty?
should you look for in a partner?
can you expect from sex?

The answers to all these questions, and many more, are supplied in this uninhibited, straight-forward, informative guide. It's ideal for teenagers who want, and need, to know about all aspects of sex.

*"One of the best books I've seen on the subject ..."* - Mary Marryat, Woman's Weekly

*"... very frank and very sensible, and occasionally funny ..."*
- Hampstead and Highgate Express

*"... detailed and helpful information about sex - including open answers to questions which many young people are afraid to ask."* - Book for Keeps

# DON'T BLAME ME – I'M A GEMINI!
## Astrology For Teenagers

## Reina James Reinstein and Mike Reinstein

Every week you probably read your stars in the magazines. They'll tell you if you're going to have a brilliant time. But astrology can tell you more - much more:

* What personality traits are associated with your Sun sign. How two people with the same sign can be opposites.
* What clothes and colours are most likely to suit you.
* How to get on with your family, friends, teachers ... and the opposite sex.
* What school subjects you are likely to excel at.

This wonderfully entertaining book also includes questionnaires to see how close you and your friends are to your Sun signs.

*"A highly entertaining guide to astrology for teenagers ..."* - Daily Telegraph

*"If you enjoy reading your stars or know a teenager who does this is an ideal gift."* - Bookshelf reviews, Stoke Newington Bookshop

*" ... a light-hearted, informative guide to astrology."* - Evening Times

# BOYS – ARE THEY REALLY ALIENS?

## Marina Gask

When it comes to understanding BOYS, girls are often left pretty confused. Aliens or not, BOYS are undeniably weird!

How come they can be quite reasonable on their own, then act like total jerks when they're with their mates?

Why do they insist on watching football all day, then talking about every detail of the match afterwards?

How can you tell if one fancies you? And how can you get one to fancy you?

Why do they get embarrassed at showing even a teeny bit of affection in public?

Boys are pretty unfathomable, but they're pretty fascinating too. Marina Gask has talked to real, live boys and has found out what every girl wants to know – what really goes on inside boys' minds, and whether they are an alien species.

*"... makes an afternoon's hilarious reading for anyone – of either sex – who knows a male between the ages of about 14 and 40."* – The Guardian Guide

*"Marina Gask has written a wonderful non-fiction book dealing with the whole subject of boys and girls ..."* – Writing Magazine

# OLIVIA

## Rosie Rushton

How much more can Olivia cope with? Her dad has gone off to live with the Wretched Rosalie - and shows no sign of coming home. Her boyfriend has dumped her and she just knows it's because she has fat thighs and freckles. Her arty mother has decided to take a zany lodger - and is very definitely being led astray by her. And to make matters worse, her best friend Poppy, who had the answers to everything, has moved to a new school.

But when drop dead gorgeous Ryan starts seriously chatting her up and her dad announces that he is coming back to Leehampton, Livi thinks that life is on the up. *But that is when the real problems start!*

*"A witty but sympathetic book,* Olivia *is a must to liven up boring Sunday afternoons!"* - Mizz

# HELP! MY FAMILY IS DRIVING ME CRAZY!
## A Survival Guide For Teenagers

## Kathryn Lamb

**Families** ...At best, they curb your lifestyle. At worst, they drive you completely crazy.

Find out the tricks that Angelica Toogood, Basil Broke, Amy Average, Steve Cash and Soumik Sen use to deal with *their* ghastly families. You'll emerge happy and healthy, with your street cred intact!

Kathryn Lamb provides some invaluable tips on how to manage your family:

Parents respond well to flattery ...
Bribery works wonders for siblings ...
Prepare for potential problems, eg. warn parents that James is 'quite artistic' (has long hair, ten earrings and a tattoo) ...
Learn the secret of really good answers – ones such as 'homework' and 'I want to be an accountant' work much better than 'nothing' or 'dunno'!

Always remember: **A happy parent is a kind and generous parent, a parent who likes to say "Yes!"**

*"An essential survival guide for all those teenagers with embarrassing/annoying parents and siblings."* – The Children's Bookseller

*"A little gem that we can all relate to. Filled with hilarious ways to get round your dreadful parents, keep them happy and live a sane life yourself! Order us a job lot now!"* – Mizz

*"It hits just the right humorous note, with case histories and tips on behaviour that are accompanied by hilarious cartoons."* – The Bookseller

## SPEAK FOR YOURSELF!
## Finding Your Voice Among Your Peers

### Rosie Rushton

Wouldn't it be wonderful to:

- * talk sensibly to the boy of your dreams?
- * think great (but true) thoughts about yourself, rather than thinking what a dork you are?
- * do what you want to do, not just what everyone else wants, or expects you to do?
- * hang out with people you really like?

Well you can! With confidence you can do anything. Here's how to get it!

*" ... combine(s) confidence building humour, factual knowledge and a real awareness of the dilemmas which young people face ... cheerfully presented, with eye-catching covers and modest price tag."* - Books for Keeps

*"... check out Rosie Rushton's brilliant new book ... a book no girl should be without."* - Shout